Profiles in Greek and Roman Mythology

ATHENA

Mitchell Lane
PUBLISHERS

P.O. Box 196
Hockessin, Delaware 19707
Visit us on the web: www.mitchelllane.com
Comments? email us: mitchelllane@mitchelllane.com

PROFILES IN GREEK AND ROMAN MYTHOLOGY

Titles in the Series

Profiles in Greek and Roman Mythology

ATHENA

Russell Roberts

Mitchell Lane
PUBLISHERS

P.O. Box 196
Hockessin, Delaware 19707
Visit us on the web: www.mitchelllane.com
Comments? email us: mitchelllane@mitchelllane.com

Printing   3   4   5   6   7   8   9

Library of Congress Cataloging-in-Publication Data
Roberts, Russell, 1953–
    Athena / By Russell Roberts.
        p. cm. — (Profiles in Greek and Roman mythology)
    Includes bibliographical references and index.
    ISBN 978-1-58415-556-0 (library bound)
    1. Athena (Greek deity)—Juvenile literature. I. Title.
BL820.M6R63 2007
398.2'0983801—dc22
                                                              2007000670

ABOUT THE AUTHOR: Russell Roberts has written and published nearly 40 books for adults and children on a variety of subjects, including baseball, memory power, business, New Jersey history, and travel. He has written numerous books for Mitchell Lane Publishers, including *Nathaniel Hawthorne*, *Thomas Jefferson*, *Holidays and Celebrations in Colonial America*, *Daniel Boone*, *The Cyclopes*, and *The Minotaur*. The contradictions of Athena have always interested him. Her mercurial personality makes her a fascinating subject to research and write about. He lives in Bordentown, New Jersey, with his family and a fat, fuzzy, and crafty calico cat named Rusti.

PHOTO CREDITS: p. 12 map—Jonathan Scott.

PUBLISHER'S NOTE: This story is based on the author's extensive research, which he believes to be accurate. Documentation of such research is contained on page 46.
    The internet sites referenced herein were active as of the publication date. Due to the fleeting nature of some web sites, we cannot guarantee they will all be active when you are reading this book.
    To reflect current usage, we have chosen to use the secular era designations BCE ("before the common era") and CE ("of the common era") instead of the traditional designations BC ("before Christ") and AD (*anno Domini,* "in the year of the Lord").

PLB / PPC2,4 / PLB2,4

TABLE OF CONTENTS

Profiles in Greek and Roman Mythology

ATHENA

In most versions of the Athena myth, the goddess is born from Zeus' head when Hephaestus (left) strikes him on the head with an ax. Zeus had commanded the god of fire to hit him to relieve a pounding headache.

ATHENA

⟨HAPTER 1

Who Is Athena?

Arachne (uh-RAK-nee) shrank back in terror. People always said that the young girl's stubborn pride would get her in trouble, but she had never believed them. Now she knew just what they meant . . . and she was scared.

She had dared to challenge a god—dared to participate in a contest with the god to see whose skill was superior. Now it was over, and guess what? The god had won. Big surprise! Gods were immortal. They had powers she could only dream of. Why had she thought she could beat this goddess in a weaving contest—that she was better on the loom than a divine being? But she had gone ahead anyway, and now . . . this! The goddess was angry—enraged at what Arachne had woven on her loom. It was a tapestry showing the gods acting foolishly: There were even scenes of Zeus disguising himself in order to trick women into being with him. Now the goddess was furious that a mere mortal had dared to show the gods acting badly. Athena's gray eyes were flashing fire, and her lips were set in a hard line.

Why did I do it? thought Arachne frantically. Why did I think I was better than she? Why did I pick this subject for my tapestry?

The goddess Athena reached for her sword, and Arachne screamed helplessly, hopelessly.

What would happen to her?

The Goddess Athena

According to Greek mythology, Athena (uh-THEE-nuh) was one of the twelve great gods and goddesses who lived on Mount Olympus and ruled the universe. The others were Zeus (ZOOS), the king of the gods and supreme ruler of the heavens; Hera (HAYR-uh), his wife and queen; Ares (AY-reez), the god of war and Hera's son; the beautiful, bewitching Aphrodite (ah-froh-DY-tee), the goddess of love; the god of fire, Hephaestus (heh-FES-tus), the one who crafted the gods' mighty weapons; fleet-footed Hermes (HUR-meez), the messenger of the gods, with wings on his shoes and helmet; Demeter (DIH-mih-ter), the goddess of the harvest; Poseidon (poh-SY-dun), the lord of the sea; the twins Apollo (ah-PAH-loh) and Artemis (AR-teh-mis), the god of light and goddess of the hunt, respectively; and gentle Dionysus (dy-oh-NY-sus), the god of wine. These eleven, along with Athena, constituted the twelve great gods and goddesses who, according to the ancient Greeks, ruled heaven and earth.

But just who was Athena—and what was her domain?

Athena was the Greek goddess of wisdom, weaving, crafts, and warfare, and a being who could be numerous things, many of them contradictory. She could be a fierce protector of those she favored during battle, a kindly friend of mortal men and women engaged in craftsmanship, or a cunning trickster and someone who would punish a mortal in the blink of an eye. She was the protector of civilized life, yet in the earliest stories about her, she is also fearsome and warlike.

Gentle protector of civilization. Warlike destroyer of cities. Friend. Foe.

Athena was a goddess of many faces. Even the story of her birth was unusual.

Birth of Athena

Zeus, the king of the gods, had a headache . . . a terrible, pounding headache that seemed determined to split open his very skull. Lying on a small couch high up on Mount Olympus, Zeus tossed and turned in agony as the headache hammered away. He wondered if it had anything to do with his swallowing of Metis (MEE-tis), his first wife. She had been the goddess of common sense, and Zeus had loved her and married her. But then Gaia (GY-uh), also known as Mother Earth, had warned him: If he and Metis had a son, the son would overthrow him, take his throne, and rule as the king of the gods in his place.

Zeus knew all about sons overthrowing their fathers. That was how he had become ruler of the gods, by leading a revolt against his father, Cronus (as Cronus had also dethroned *his* father, Uranus [YOO-ruh-nus]). Zeus did not take Gaia's warning lightly, yet he needed the wise advice that Metis provided. What should he do?

After much thought, Zeus decided to trick Metis. He suggested to her that they play a game in which they each assumed different shapes. Metis agreed, and began turning herself into various creatures big and small. When she became a tiny fly, Zeus quickly opened his mouth and swallowed her. She did not go to his stomach, but to his head, from where she continued to advise him.

A while after Zeus did this, his head began to hurt. Eventually he was in agony, and his cries of pain brought the other gods hurrying to his side. There was nothing they could do to ease his suffering. Little did they know that the cause of his discomfort was Metis. She was indeed going to have a child, but it was going to be a girl, not a boy. To prepare for the baby's birth, she sat inside Zeus' head, hammering out a helmet and weaving a beautiful robe. It was her hammering that was causing Zeus' headache.

At last Zeus could take no more. He called for his son Hephaestus to help him. Hephaestus, the god of fire, was an expert at the forge and metalworking. As the other gods stood stunned, Zeus commanded Hephaestus to split open his skull with one of the heavy axes that he used at the forge.

At first Hephaestus would not do this, because to strike Zeus was unthinkable. But the king of the gods roared that if his son would not obey him, he would toss him out of Olympus and up into the vast reaches of the universe.

With no choice but to obey, Hephaestus selected his best bronze ax and struck Zeus on the skull with it. On earth, people looked to the heavens as the thunderous sound rolled down from the mountains and across the land, and agreed that the gods were angry.

In fact, the gods were not angry—they were amazed. For when Hephaestus struck Zeus, his mighty skull split open and out of it stepped a young woman wearing the armor and robe that Metis had made for her. The woman was the goddess Athena. Zeus, his headache gone and suffering no ill effects from the ax blow, made room for Athena on Mount Olympus. She took her place among the immortals, where she quickly became Zeus' favorite daughter.

A variation on this story comes from the Greek island of Crete. This version claims that Athena had not been inside Zeus' head, but rather was hiding in a nearby cloud. When Zeus struck the cloud with his head, Athena stepped out. Because this event was supposed to have taken place near a stream called the Triton, Athena was sometimes called Athena Tritogeneia (try-tuh-jeh-NY-uh, "born of Triton"[1]). As a further explanation of this birth, it was sometimes said that Poseidon, who was the father of the river god Triton, was also her father.

The story of Athena emerging from her father's skull is the most common account of her birth in Greek mythology. Because of her role as a warrior, she is usually pictured as wearing a helmet and a breastplate (armor for the upper body) called the aegis. On it is the head of the Gorgon Medusa (muh-DOO-suh), complete with snakes for hair. (How she obtained that head is told in chapter 4 of this book.) She also carries a shield. Athena's eyes are gray. As Edith Hamilton, one of the foremost Greek mythology experts, said: "The word oftenest used to describe her is 'gray-eyed,' or, as it is sometimes translated, 'flashing-eyed.'"[2]

Sometimes she is accompanied by Nike (NY-kee), the goddess of victory. The ancient Greek writer Homer also indicates that Athena had a cap that made her invisible. When she wore it no one could see her, not even other gods. She was, indeed, a unique being.

Homer

Homer is credited with writing two of the most famous poems in history—*Iliad* and *Odyssey*—and both are a foundation of Greek mythology. But did Homer really exist? Almost nothing is known about the person named Homer (if indeed there was a person named Homer). He is said to have been Greek, he may have lived in the eighth century BCE, and he may have been blind. That is the extent of the personal information on Homer.

Bust of Homer

According to one theory, Homer was not one person, but actually a group of poets known as the Homeridae. These were men who were not sent into battle because their loyalty as soldiers was uncertain. Thus it became their task to remember events and memorize poetry, and then to sing about these events in the form of a poem. (This was before a literary tradition—writing such things down—was practiced.) *Homer* could have come from the name of this group of poets.

There is some question about whether the same person wrote both *Iliad* and *Odyssey* because the tales are so radically different. The *Iliad* is more of an emotional work, featuring people (and gods) caught up in the workings of the world with no escape. The *Odyssey*, on the other hand, is more like a typical modern story: The hero undertakes a journey, faces villains, and in the end defeats them.

Because the world Homer describes is real, not fictional, some scholars contend that he was a real person. He could have lived, and if he did, his work takes on more importance as a "historical snapshot." Theories continue to abound as to the actual identity of Homer, and whether he—or someone else, or a lot of someones—wrote these two great classics of literature. Homer's identity is likely to remain a mystery for many more years.

Rome

Black Sea

Greece

The Dardanelles

Troy

Turkey

Sparta

Athens

Mediterranean Sea

Crete

Persia

Lake Triton

Libya

Africa

Athena may have been worshiped in Libya, Africa, before she became a deity in Greece. She was said to have been born in Lake Triton. In Greece, the myth evolved, and she became the patron goddess of Athens. Eventually the Romans also incorporated her into their religion, where she was called Minerva.

ATHENA

CHAPTER 2

Origins of Athena

There are several different theories about Athena's background before the Greeks came to regard her as a major goddess. One is that she was a weather goddess. Another theory is that Athena was an owl, or perhaps a bird goddess. This relationship might explain why she took on certain shapes in Greek mythology. For instance, in Homer's epic poem *Odyssey*, she appears as a sea eagle. At other points she takes the form of an owl.

Yet it was not only bird shapes that Athena could assume. Again in the *Odyssey*, she disguises herself as a young shepherd boy. In the encounter with Arachne, she takes the form of an old woman.

Some scholars believe that the idea of Athena comes from the region of Lake Triton, an ancient lake in Libya in Africa. Even the great philosopher Plato believed Athena to be from this area. "Plato, too, assigned a Libyan genesis [point of origin] to Athena, identifying her with the goddess Neith, who reigned in a period before paternity [the idea that a god needed a father] was recognized,"[1] said Athena researcher Lee Hall.

The theory of Athena's African origins is given further believability by the fact that *Athena* is not a Greek name. Some believe that her name is Libyan. Athena's warrior nature was supposedly celebrated in Libya in annual festivals during which girls or possibly virgin priestesses divided into two groups and fought each other. The winner became high priestess.

According to this theory, Africans migrating to Crete took Athena with them. Indeed, Crete appears to be unique among many other cultures of that time. Said Hall: "The . . . inhabitants of Crete appear . . . to have practiced rituals associated with a female deity or deities."[2] He

goes on to note that evidence of Athena's existence on Crete can still be found at some ancient sites, such as caves or mountains.[3]

From Crete, Athena's worship was brought to mainland Greece, and her birth story evolved into the one that became the most popular—that of her stepping from Zeus' head. Pottery findings indicate there was a migration of Libyans into Crete around 4000 BCE. If so, it would further reinforce the origin of Athena as Libyan, and that she was an African goddess long before she was adopted by Greek mythology.

If any of these African backgrounds for Athena are true, then she was actually worshiped long before the common story of her birth from the head of Zeus evolved. Thus, even though she became Zeus's daughter in Greek myth, Athena's story may have been older than the story of her father.

Another fascinating theory about the relationship between Zeus and Athena is that the two were initially lovers, not father and daughter, and that Athena was the far more important god, while Zeus was just a minor deity. This theory speculates that the relationship between the two was changed to father and daughter only because of the male-dominated society in ancient Greece.[4]

Women's Role in Greek Society
No matter which story of her birth is believed, it seems that the primary one—that of her stepping out from Zeus' head—is an attempt by Greek storytellers to remove her femininity. Even though Metis may have been pregnant, Athena did not need to be born from a woman's womb. Ancient Greece was a patriarchal society in which women did not usually play a major role. In war, politics, the economy, and all else, men were the masters, and women were given secondary status. Women were not considered to be full citizens in Greek society.

There are several reasons for a woman's lesser status. One was that, long before a woman's critical role in reproduction was known, it was thought that the male was responsible for all the vital ingredients for making babies. A woman was considered to be merely a receptacle for the male seed. This idea probably came from agriculture, where the earth (considered female) awaited a male farmer to plant seeds in order to produce crops. The male was fertilizing the earth, just like a human male fertilized a female.

But there was more to it than that. The story of Pandora (pan-DOR-uh) played into this "anti-women" feeling as well. According to the tale, Zeus gave Pandora—the first woman—to Epimetheus as a gift. Epimetheus, who forgot that his brother Prometheus had warned him not to take gifts from Zeus, took Pandora as his bride. When he did so, the jar that was her dowry opened, and out came all the evils that would plague mankind—including old age, jealousy, greed, and disease. Because of this "gift," women were considered responsible for all of man's suffering.[5]

Pandora was a gift from Zeus to man. Zeus wanted to balance out the gift of fire, given to man by Prometheus, by giving him Pandora and her jar, or box, of evils.

The Greeks' attitude toward women could be seen in their feelings about courage. Only men, it was thought, had the courage and bravery to go to war. Although they acknowledged, for example, that it took courage for a woman to defend her family from intruders while her husband was away, that type of action was not considered the same as marching out to meet the enemy on the battlefield. As Hall wrote: "From the first moment she emerged from Zeus's head, Athena personified the masculine virtues of valor. . . . Athena's birth signified the triumph of male over female . . . femininity was weakness, masculinity, power."[6]

In ancient Greek society, a woman was condemned by biology, by her supposed psychological inadequacy, and by tradition to assume a lesser role in Greek life. On the other hand, there was Athena, a female warrior goddess. When Athena was given credit for helping the Greeks defeat the Persian Empire during the Persian Wars (490 and 480–479 BCE), they had to explain how she was different. She had to have been born from a man.

The Virgin Goddess

Athena was known by several different names, each describing one of her specific characteristics or traits. These names are known as epithets. For example, she was a protector of city life, and so was called Athena Polias, or "Athena of the City."

Another unique characteristic of Athena was that she never had a lover or a mate: She was always a virgin. Thus she was sometimes called Pallas Athena, which roughly translates into "Athena the Maiden." By rejecting the common female roles of lover and wife, Athena was reinforcing the male attributes of her personality and downplaying her female side.

There are two stories that also link the term *Pallas* to Athena. The first involves Pallas, a hideous winged monster. He tried to attack Athena, but the goddess fought him off. She killed him and made her famous aegis out of his skin.

Another story concerns a female companion named Pallas, who was the daughter of the river god Triton. One day the two girls were playing a game of war when Athena accidentally killed Pallas with a spear thrust. This happened because Zeus, seeing that the game was getting too violent, tried to protect both women by placing his aegis between them. Instead, he only managed to distract Pallas, which set her up for the fatal thrust by Athena.

As she was crying over her mistake and grieving for her friend, Athena thought she saw a likeness of Pallas on the trunk of a felled tree. She ran to the spot and pulled away the plants and branches that surrounded the tree trunk, thus freeing her friend's likeness. That is the reason she is the goddess of carvers and sculptors—because she understood how to free beauty from a natural material, such as wood or stone.

As a gift to her fallen friend's memory, this likeness of Pallas was decreed by Athena to have special powers. It would help and protect anyone who sought safety in its presence. Athena placed it next to Zeus' throne on Mount Olympus. On earth, mortals knew that the figure of Pallas brought good luck to anyone who touched it. Wood and stone copies of the figure of Pallas were kept by many who sought Athena's blessing.

Athens

The gods of Greek myth were frequently at odds with each other. They argued and fought and sometimes behaved illogically. Humans could never be certain how the gods would react to them—or whether their punishments would be fair. To try to stay on the good side of at least one god, each city dedicated itself to a particular guardian or protector god. For Athens, that protector was Athena.

Before the place was named, both Athena and Poseidon favored the area that would become Athens. Since both of these gods wanted to be the god of that region, they decided to hold a contest. They would each give the people there a gift. Whoever gave the gift that the people preferred would be the winner.

Poseidon went first. He struck the ground with his mighty trident and a great spring gushed forth. But the water produced by the spring was salty and not good for drinking.

Then it was Athena's turn. From the ground of the Acropolis (a large, high hill in town), she caused an olive tree to sprout and bloom. The olive would provide food, fuel (from the oil), and wood. The people chose the olive tree as their preferred gift, and Athena became the god of the city that would take her name—Athens.

According to Edith Hamilton, this contest had unfortunate results for women. At the time, women, who outnumbered men by one, were allowed to vote. All the women voted for Athena's gift, while all the

men voted for Poseidon's. This made the women and Athena the victor. In anger, the men took the right to vote away from women.[7]

When Athena became the goddess of what would be known as Athens, the city began its rise in importance. Ultimately it became one of the leading Greek city-states and, during much of the fifth century BCE, was a world power.

Athena was the ideal god for Athens. More than any other of the Olympians, she represented the superiority of the male over the female. This is exactly the society that emerged in Athens. Women were denied citizenship and essentially belonged to men like any other object. By having Athena as their patron god, Athens was confirming that their society was correct in its unequal treatment of men and women. Despite this approach, Athens began to build the civilization that is still remembered and celebrated today, thousands of years after its heyday.

The Glory of Athens

Athens began its rise to power with the reforms instituted by a man named Solon. Before he became chief magistrate of Athens in 594 BCE, the city was in crisis. It had been led by a council of nine elders, who were members of the aristocracy. The common people had few rights. They had no say in how they were governed. They were supposed to sit back and await the decisions of the aristocrats, who supposedly knew what was best.

The common people were unhappy with this system, and their agitation led to Solon's appointment as magistrate. Bowing to the will of the people—an act that many see as forming the first pillars of democracy—Solon rewrote the constitution to give others a say in government. He established law courts that instituted trial by jury. He also created a council (called the *boule*) and an assembly (known as the *ekklesia*) of numerous members. These were the main political bodies. They ensured that more than just a few people would participate in the political process in Athens. Solon also tried to help farmers who were in debt to the rich and in danger of losing their land to them. He encouraged industrial growth in the city by instituting citizenship to skilled foreigners. By reforming the political, legal, and economic processes, Solon had an impact on virtually everyone in Athens.

Reproduction of Ancient Athens, Greece

If Solon laid the foundation for greater participation by citizens, then Cleisthenes was the one who built the house of Athenian democracy. Beginning around 509 BCE, Cleisthenes instituted a series of reforms that allowed all Athenian citizens to participate in the political process. Previously, there had been four tribes, or groups of aristocrats, that had been in charge of governing. Cleisthenes replaced them with ten new tribes, or villages. Each tribe drew members from one of three geographical areas: the city, the coast, or inland. Each tribe then sent 50 members to the boule, which became the main governing body and voted on all matters of national concern for the growing city. The result was that ordinary male citizens, rather than just the aristocrats, could vote and decide matters that affected their daily lives.

Under this system Athens rose to its greatest glory. In particular, under a leader named Pericles, Athens became a world power. In 477 BCE it established the Delian League, which was a confederation of Greek city-states that sought to defend itself against the expanding Persian Empire. Because Athens was the leading sea power in Greece, it became the leader of the Delian League, which at one time had more than 200 members. Most of the members made financial contributions to Athens; in return, Athens would defend them from enemies. With its unrivaled fleet, Athens became a major military power.

With all this money flowing into its treasury, Athens grew quite rich. When Pericles came to power around 461 BCE, he launched an ambitious building program. He restored temples destroyed in

previous wars and had new ones constructed, including the famous Parthenon.

The Parthenon still stands today. It is a symbol of Athena's glory and a testimony to the esteem in which the Athenians held the goddess. Built between 447 BCE and 432 BCE and dedicated to Athena Parthenos—Athena the Virgin—the temple features sculpture that tells several stories from her life. One is the story of her birth from Zeus' head; another relates her victory over Poseidon concerning Athens. The Parthenon was considered the finest example of Greek architecture, even in its day. Buildings such as this helped make Athens one of the most magnificent cities in the ancient world.

The Acropolis was where Athena ruled supreme. A thirty-foot-high statue of her overlooked a walkway that people used for making sacrifices and offerings to her. The statue, wearing a helmet and carrying a shield and spear, was a reminder that Athena brought victory to Athens.

Yet Athens was more than just a military power and home of temples. It became a home of culture and thought—an intellectual bastion. Plays were produced in the theater of Dionysus. Scientists used math to predict such events as the movements of the moon. The great philosopher Socrates roamed the streets, urging the people he encountered to examine their lives and to seek the truth in all matters. In a world that was often unbelievably cruel, Athens was a civilized society. A lover of literature one minute, a fighter the next—that was the typical Athenian.

Ultimately, however, the glory faded. Athens was defeated by its arch-rival, the city-state Sparta, in the Peloponnesian War (431–404 BCE), and began its decline as a great power. But while it lasted, Athens was like a world unto itself, a world that is still celebrated today as a model of enlightened thought and culture. Athens was a city just like its goddess—both warring and civilized. Because of the many blessings she brought to the city, the Athenians celebrated their goddess with several festivals.

The Festivals of Athena

The Arrephoria: The Arrephoria was held in midsummer. Two seven-year-old girls were selected to live near Athena's temple and assist her priestesses for one year. They carried baskets containing secret holy objects down from the Acropolis to a place called Aphrodite in the Gardens. There they would get two more baskets, which they'd give to Athena's priestesses. Then the girls were dismissed and two others replaced them. It is thought that the ceremony represented the journey for females from wisdom (Athena) to love (Aphrodite).

The Chalkeia: The Chalkeia, held every fourth year before the Panathenaea (see below), called for women to weave a robe showing the battle between the Giants and Zeus, among other events. The robe was then presented to Athena in her temple. The statue of Athena was dressed in this robe ten months later at the Plynteria. This festival is thought to honor Athena's protection of crafts and craftspeople.

The Plynteria: The Plynteria, also known as the feast of the bath, occurred when the statue of Athena Polias was brought to the sea and washed. While the statue was gone, her temple was scrubbed spotless. A group of women carried the statue, which was apparently clothed and wearing jewelry, to the ocean. There they undressed it and washed it. Only these women were allowed to see the statue without clothing.

The Panathenaea: The major festival for Athena and one of the most spectacular in ancient Greece, the Panathenaea centered around the goddess's birthday. It was likely held for five days or more in July or August. It featured athletic contests, poetry recitals, and musical contests that included dancing. Contest winners were

Panathenaea games

given a crown of olive leaves, as well as vases filled with olive oil. The women made a garment to present to the statue of Athena Polias on her birthday. (Every fourth year, a gigantic garment was taken to the Acropolis and presented to the statue of Athena Parthenos in the Parthenon.) Cakes and other offerings were also brought, as well as many sacrificial animals. The festival ended with a feast throughout the city.

The Fable of Arachne, a 1657 painting by Diego Rodriguez de Silva y Velásquez. In the background, Athena, in an ancient helmet, wields her sword, while Arachne weaves in front of her. Scholars believe that Athena is also in the foreground, disguised as an old woman (at the spinning wheel).

ATHENA

CHAPTER 3

The Angry Athena

Arachne bent over her loom, weaving another masterpiece out of wool. When she was finished, she held it up for all to see. The people who were watching her applauded. Truly the tapestry she had woven of a forest and a gurgling brook was gorgeous. She had used several different colors in her picture—to show the trees, water, and ground. The places where she had joined the colored threads together looked seamless. It was like a painting made of wool: The colors were beautiful and rich, and the objects vivid and lifelike.

No matter what Arachne wove on her loom, it always turned out to be wonderful. Clothes, blankets, tapestries . . . it didn't matter. They were always lovely, always impeccably made. She was somehow able to work the raw wool with her fingers, kneading it and shaping it, until it was as light and fluffy as a cloud. When she spun the wool and ran it through her loom, it was soft and easy to work with. Her embroidery added the finishing touch. When she displayed the finished product, it was an absolute masterpiece, a stunning combination of craftsmanship and artistic vision.

People came from far and wide to watch Arachne work her magic on the loom. They agreed that there was no finer weaver than Arachne in all of Greece—perhaps in all the world.

Arachne became used to hearing people lavishly praise her work. In fact, she heard it so often that Arachne herself began to believe all the wonderful things that were said about her. She began to think that she did not have an equal on the loom *anywhere*—not on earth or in the heavens.

One day, when someone made the comment that no one could spin as well as Arachne, not even the goddess Athena, the mortal girl

nodded in agreement. She felt that not even Athena could beat her in a contest.

Athena, as the goddess of weaving and crafts, had taught many Greeks the art of weaving and the talents of creating through crafts-manship. All Arachne had to do was acknowledge that her skill at the loom was a gift from Athena, and everybody would have understood. But with incredible hubris, Arachne had declared that she was greater than the goddess herself.

When Athena heard the girl's comment, she was displeased. She was very proud of her weaving skills. Among the gods, Athena's talent at the loom was legendary. One of the objects she had made for the gods was a gorgeous veil and headdress for Hera, the wife of Zeus.

Naturally Athena thought of herself as the best weaver, and Arach-ne's comments infuriated her. Athena came down to earth from Mount Olympus, disguised herself as an old woman, and went to see Arachne.

She found the girl weaving at her loom in a pleasant, shady grove of trees. Arachne was alone this day, but quite used to having people watch her weave. When the old woman suddenly showed up and watched her work, the young girl did not think it odd.

After watching Arachne, the old woman complimented her on her skill but cautioned her not to be so boastful. *Surely there is someone your equal*, the old woman said. When Arachne asked her whom she meant, the old woman mentioned the goddess Athena.

Then Arachne made a critical mistake. She laughed scornfully at the mention of Athena and boasted that not even she could match her skill. She added that if Athena were there now, she would challenge her to a contest to see who was the better weaver.

With that, Athena threw off her disguise, revealing herself to the girl. The contest was on.

Perhaps foolishly, Arachne was not afraid. Another loom was set up in the grove of trees, and the two began weaving tapestries. When Athena had finished, hers was a masterpiece. In the center it depicted many of the gods on Mount Olympus, such as Zeus and Poseidon. In the corners were small pictures showing incidents in which mortals had tried to prove themselves better than the gods, and of the terrible fate that had befallen them.

Then she looked at Arachne's work. The girl's tapestry was filled with incidents that showed the gods acting less than honorably. One scene showed Zeus entering a tower as a golden shower in order to seduce a woman whom her father had tried to protect. Another scene was of Zeus again, this time disguised as a swan so that he could trick a married woman named Leda (LEE-duh) into sleeping with him.

Arachne's tapestry was beautiful, and the figures seemed almost as if they would begin speaking at any moment—but everything that was portrayed showed foolish gods. Arachne was mocking them.

Athena drew her sword. Arachne shrank back in fear, but Athena had not meant the sword for her. Angrily, the goddess slashed Arachne's tapestry in half. Then she touched Arachne on the forehead. Immediately the girl was overwhelmed by shame. She realized how poorly she had acted, and how she had dared compare herself to the gods. So great was her guilt that she left the grove and hanged herself.

When Athena saw the girl's lifeless body hanging from a tree, she took pity on her. She decided to restore life to Arachne, but she also never wanted her behavior to be forgotten. As Arachne returned to life, her body began to shrink. Her hair, nose, and ears fell off. Her head shrank, and her fingers went to both sides of her body, where they grew into small legs. Where a human had once been, there was now a spider, whose body was full of thread for weaving its web. Athena had condemned the girl and her descendants to an eternity of spinning and weaving. Sometimes the spider is able to simply hang down by a single thread—so that it can remember how Arachne had once swung from a tree for her treatment of the gods.

Teiresias

As Arachne discovered, Athena's vengeance could be terrible indeed. Another who found this out was Teiresias (ty-REE-see-uhs).

One day he was out walking when he accidentally stumbled upon Athena bathing naked in a clear pool. The goddess was extremely sensitive about her maidenhood. As Greek mythology expert Paul Hamlyn observed, "Woe to anyone who wounded her modesty!"[1] Feeling his eyes upon her, Athena swung around. Furious that Teiresias had seen her undressed, she splashed water upon his face, blinding him.

Chariclo, the mother of Teiresias, begged Athena to have mercy. After all, she pointed out, her son had not meant to see Athena; it had been an accident. But gods usually do not admit that they are wrong, and this time was no exception. She refused to undo her punishment of Teiresias. However, perhaps she did feel that she had been too harsh with him, for she took the snake off her aegis and told it to lick his ears. When it did, Teiresias received the gift of prophecy. He became famous for his ability to foretell the future, and he played a role in several other Greek tales.

Athena and Hera

Because Athena had been born from Zeus, technically Hera was her mother, because Hera was the wife of Zeus. Even so, there was no mother-daughter bond between Hera and Athena.

"Athena despised Hera as thoroughly as Hera detested Athena,"[2] wrote Lee Hall.

Hera was an extraordinarily jealous goddess. She knew that Zeus, although married to her, was attracted to human females and had affairs with them. Often he used trickery to gain their love, such as when he assumed the shape of another woman's husband in order to get her to love him. Trickery or not, it did not matter to Hera; she was very jealous of all the women with whom Zeus had affairs, and she often punished them.

Because Athena had no surviving mother, there was no other woman at whom Hera could direct her jealousy. However, relations were still cool between the two. If Athena was the "non-woman," Hera represented what the Greeks considered to be the "typical woman." She was jealous, suspicious, a schemer, and a nag.

Hephaestus triumphantly returns to Mount Olympus. Jealous Hera tried to produce a child without Zeus just as Zeus had produced Athena without her. The child, Hephaestus, was born lame and ugly, so Hera cast him off Mount Olympus. To punish her, Hephaestus made her a cursed throne. Once she sat upon it (right), she could not get up. He set her free only when she let him return to Olympus.

Hera, jealous of Zeus for producing Athena without her, then produced Hephaestus, the god of fire. When Hephaestus was born ugly and lame, Hera wanted no parts of him. She threw him off Mount Olympus and into the sea, where he lived for nine years and became an expert at the forge. Ultimately he got back at Hera by earning a seat on Mount Olympus, where he lived as one of the twelve immortal gods. This is why he was present when Zeus had his headache. (Of course, this means that his birth came *before* Athena's, rather than after hers, as the story would indicate, for it was Athena's birth that Hera sought to duplicate. But Greek mythology does not often follow a neat chronological order.)

Athena Punishes Ajax

Ajax was a mighty warrior for the Greeks during the Trojan War. When Odysseus (oh-DIH-see-us) was given the armor of the great warrior

According to Homer's *Iliad*, the Trojan War was more than a battle between men. The gods also played major roles. Ajax (center, left) battled the mighty Trojan warrior, Hector. Athena stands behind Ajax, and Apollo, with his bow and laurel wreath, aids Hector.

Achilles (uh-KIH-leez), who had fallen in battle, Ajax got angry. He considered himself twice the fighter that Odysseus was, and he wanted that armor. He decided to take revenge against Odysseus and other Greeks for denying him the honor.

But Odysseus was Athena's favorite, so she decided to punish Ajax for his attitude. She made him go insane, then watched as he wandered into the pen of goats and sheep that were intended as food for the Greeks. In his insanity, Ajax began killing the animals, thinking that he was killing Greeks. Then Athena removed the madness from his mind, and Ajax saw the terrible thing that he had done—killing poor defenseless animals not for food, but just to kill.

"The poor cattle," he said, "killed to no purpose by my hand."[3]

Driven by his guilt, Ajax committed suicide by throwing himself on his sword. He had learned what Arachne and Teiresias had found out—it was dangerous to anger Athena.

Teiresias

Teiresias was perhaps the most famous prophet in Greek mythology. However, the way he received the gift of second sight—indeed, even the way he was blinded—is explained two different ways. Besides being a prophet, he also experienced life as both a man and a woman.

The first story about how Teiresias lost his sight is related above: He stumbled upon Athena taking a bath, and she blinded him. Feeling merciful, she gave him the gift of second sight.

Another story has to do with the continuing rivalry between married couple Zeus and Hera. According to this legend, Teiresias was out for a stroll when he came upon two snakes that were wrapped together. Outraged, he hit the two snakes sharply with his staff.

His actions may have pleased him, but they angered Hera. The goddess of marriage and childbirth, she protected unions between male and female members of any species, even between snakes. To punish Teiresias, she turned him into a woman.

Teiresias lived as a woman for several years; she even married a man and had children with him. One day, while out on another stroll, Teiresias once again came upon two snakes that were mating. Some sources say she hit the snakes again; others say she left them alone. Either way, Hera turned Teiresias back into a man.

All should have been well, but then Teiresias was asked to settle an argument between Zeus and Hera about whether it was more pleasurable to be a man or a woman, because he had experienced life as both. When Teiresias revealed how much more physical pleasure a woman can experience, Hera struck him blind. Zeus could not undo Hera's action, so he gave Teiresias the gift of prophecy.

Teiresias appears in many other Greek myths. He helps Odysseus in Hades, he argues for allowing the worship of the new god Dionysus in Thebes, and he reveals to Oedipus (EH-dih-pus) that he has unwittingly killed his father and married his mother.

Teiresias and Odysseus (seated)

Perseus holding the head of the Gorgon Medusa after he had cut it off. He was only able to defeat her because he received help from both Hermes and Athena.

ATHENA

CHAPTER 4
Athena and Heroes

As the warrior goddess, Athena stood beside the heroic, whether they were engaged in battle or some other quest. Thus she aided Heracles (HAYR-uh-kleez)—also known by his Roman name of Hercules (HER-kyoo-leez)—as he completed his legendary twelve labors, helping him several times. It was also she who welcomed Heracles to Mount Olympus, where he ascended after his death.

Among other heroes she helped, two names stand out: Perseus (PUR-see-uhs) and Odysseus.

The Tale of Perseus

King Acrisius (uh-KRIH-see-us) of Argos had been warned that his beautiful daughter Danae (DAA-nah-ee) would have a son that would cause his death. The only way for Acrisius to avoid this fate was to kill his daughter. The king knew that the gods would be very angry with him if he killed his own child, so instead he built a house of bronze, sank it underground, and imprisoned Danae in it so that no man could ever marry and conceive a child with her.

But Acrisius hadn't considered Zeus. The king of the gods had seen Danae and fallen in love with her. He transformed himself into a shower of gold and fell from the sky into the bronze house. As a result of their union, Danae had a baby boy, whom she named Perseus.

For a time Danae tried to keep her son's identity a secret, but eventually Acrisius found out. He was terrified of the boy, but could not kill him for the same reason he could not kill Danae. However, he could do the next best thing: He could put them where they would probably die. He built a giant chest, locked Danae and Perseus in it, and had it tossed into the sea.

Luck was with them, however, because the chest came ashore on an island. There it was found by a kindly fisherman named Dictys (DIK-tis). He took the young woman and her baby back to his home, where they lived happily for many years.

Eventually trouble returned. The ruler of the island, Polydectes (pah-lee-DEK-teez), fell in love with Danae but wanted nothing to do with Perseus, who was by this time fully grown. Polydectes plotted his death, and came up with a way to get rid of Perseus.

The ruler announced that he was to be married. He held a big celebration, to which all the guests brought expensive gifts. Perseus, who was poor, brought nothing. Humiliated, the young man cried out that he would bring him a gift better than all others—the head of Medusa.

Polydectes smiled secretly, because this is exactly what he had hoped Perseus would say. Medusa was a Gorgon, a hideous monster who had live snakes for hair. She was so ugly that anyone who looked at her turned to stone.

Ironically, Medusa was once a beautiful woman. But one night, she made the mistake of taking Poseidon as a lover in Athena's temple. Athena, furious that Medusa would defile her temple in that way, transformed Medusa so that, according to mythologist Hall, "her teeth were so large that she could not close her mouth . . . her ugly tongue lolled on her coarse lips. Snakes . . . wreathed her face."[1] (This is another illustration of how risky it was to get Athena angry!) It was certain death to try to defeat her, but that was what rash Perseus had promised to do.

Perseus immediately went searching for Medusa. He did not know where she was, so he spent much time trying to locate her. On his travels he met Hermes, the messenger of the gods, who agreed to help him. He also gave Perseus a special sword that would not break.

Perseus was just wondering how he could get close enough to Medusa to use the special sword when he encountered another god. It was Athena in all her radiant beauty, wearing her helmet and holding a spear. The gray-eyed goddess smiled at Perseus, and then gave him a shining bronze shield.

The Head of Medusa, by Peter Paul Rubens, painted around 1618. The Gorgon Medusa, with her hair of snakes, was able to turn people to stone even after her death. Perseus gave the head to Athena, and she wore it on her aegis.

"Look into this when you attack the Gorgon," she said. "You will be able to see her in it as in a mirror, and so avoid her deadly power."[2]

Now Perseus had hope, thanks to Athena. Then Hermes told him that to fight the Gorgon he would also need winged sandals, a magic wallet that would always be the right size for whatever was placed in it, and a cap that made the person who wore it invisible.

After Perseus obtained these things, Hermes led him to the island where Medusa lived with her two Gorgon sisters. They were asleep when he found them. Then Athena once again appeared at his side. As he floated above the Gorgons in his winged sandals, looking at them only with Athena's shield, the two gods told Perseus which sister was Medusa.

Just as Perseus was about to strike, Athena guided his hand. With one stroke of the mighty blade, Medusa's head came off. Perseus grabbed it and put it into the magic wallet. The sound woke up the other two Gorgons, but they couldn't see Perseus because he was

As one of the most popular figures in Greek mythology, Athena had many temples dedicated to her. The most famous is the Parthenon in Athens. It was erected in honor of Athena's virginal status.

wearing the cap that made him invisible. He then flew away with Medusa's head safely in his wallet.

On his way back to his home, Perseus had another adventure. He rescued a beautiful young woman named Andromeda from being eaten by a sea monster; ultimately he would marry her.

When he arrived back home, he found the wicked king Polydectes giving a banquet. His mother had refused to marry him and had hid in an island temple to try to escape the man. When Perseus arrived at the banquet hall, all eyes were drawn to him, because no one thought he would still be alive. Perseus snatched Medusa's head out of his wallet, taking care not to look at it himself. The head turned everyone else in the hall, including Polydectes, into stone.

At that point Athena appeared before him once again. Perseus gave her Medusa's head. There was a blinding explosion of light, and then the head of Medusa was part of the breastplate, or aegis, that Athena always wore.

Later on, when Perseus was taking part in a discus-throwing contest, his discus accidentally flew into the crowd and killed Acrisius, Danae's father. The prophecy had come true after all. Thereafter Perseus, Danae, and Andromeda lived happily for the rest of their days. Undoubtedly, Perseus never forgot the time when the great goddess Athena helped him kill the Gorgon Medusa.

Athena and Odysseus

In the epic struggle between Greeks and Trojans known as the Trojan War, Athena—who favored the Greeks—had one particular favorite hero among all the Greek warriors. It was Odysseus, whom the Romans would call Ulysses. He possessed both cunning and courage, two of the traits she admired most in humans. In Homer's epic poem *Iliad*, which tells the story of the Trojan War, Athena plays a prominent role.

At one point the great Greek hero Achilles, who is mad at the Greek king Agamemnon (aa-guh-MEM-non), refuses to fight the Trojans. Seeing their mightiest warrior act this way, the other Greeks talk seriously of returning home. Unwilling to let her Trojan enemies win, Athena speaks so that only Odysseus can hear.

"Don't give up," the goddess of war tells Odysseus, urging him to move among the troops. "Use your powers to persuade them with winning words to leave their ships beached, and prepare to fight and be heroes."[3]

Odysseus does exactly that, and the men rally. The war is back on, and Athena is pleased.

At another point during a battle, Odysseus is surrounded by Trojan soldiers. Although the Trojans hack at him with spears and swords,

The Trojans pull the giant wooden horse left by the Greeks into their walled city. Hiding in the belly of the horse are Greek soldiers, who will slip out at night and let their comrades into the unsuspecting city. This trick enables the Greeks to win the Trojan War.

they cannot touch him, and Odysseus knows that Athena is protecting him. When a Trojan does wound Odysseus, it is not fatal, because Athena prevents the wound from hitting any vital organs. In the end, other Greeks come to Odysseus' rescue and carry him away in their chariot to safety. Odysseus knows that he is alive only because Athena wishes him to be.

At the end of the war, a group of soldiers, led by Odysseus, hides in the belly of a gigantic wooden horse. A messenger tells the Trojans it is a gift from Athena, and the Trojans pull it within the walls of their city. That night the Greeks pour out of the horse and let their comrades in. Troy is conquered. Athena, the goddess of cunning, came up with the plan, but Odysseus also claimed credit for the deception. These are just a few of the times Athena helped Odysseus.

The Trojan War

The Trojan War is the kind of war about which epic tales are told. But did it really happen?

Archaeologists believe that Troy was a city located in modern-day Turkey. The city was extremely wealthy, partially because it controlled shipping traffic through the Dardanelles, a narrow straight in north-western Turkey that connects the Aegean Sea with the Sea of Marmara. The Greeks wanted to attack Troy probably because it was wealthy or to end its commercial domination of the Dardanelles.

Legend tells a different reason for the war. A golden apple inscribed "for the fairest" was tossed into a wedding by Eris, the goddess of discord. Paris, the prince of Troy, was given the dubious honor of deciding for whom the apple was meant. Aphrodite, goddess of love, promised him the love of the most beautiful woman on earth if he chose her as "the fairest." Athena and Hera also offered him bribes. When Paris awarded the apple to Aphrodite, she gave him Helen of Troy, wife of Greek King Menelaus (and made a lasting enemy of Athena for the Trojans). Paris took Helen to Troy, and the Greeks came after him.

The Greek military expedition included many famous warriors, such as Achilles, Ajax, Nestor, and Odysseus. The campaign against Troy lasted ten years. The first nine were marked by relative inactivity. Troy was a walled city, and heavily defended. Finally Achilles killed the great Trojan hero Hector, and Paris killed Achilles. Odysseus (with Athena's help) came up with the idea of smuggling Greek soldiers into the city in the belly of a giant wooden horse, and then emerging in the middle of the night. The plan worked. When the Trojans brought the horse into the city, the Greeks slipped out of it at night, let the other Greek soldiers in, and ransacked the city. Only a few Trojans survived the massacre.

The return home of Odysseus and some of the other Greek warriors provided the inspiration for Homer's epic poem *Odyssey*.

The Burning of Troy

Gaia hands Erichthonius to Athena. Athena's maternal instinct, very rarely seen, surfaces when her son Erichthonius is born. She brings the baby to three sisters, but ultimately must take him back and raise him herself.

ATHENA

CHAPTER 5

Other Tales of Athena

As one of the best-known gods, Athena was a popular figure in Greek myth. She appeared in many stories. The following are just a few of those tales.

Athena's Child

Athena certainly displayed many masculine qualities. Her aegis was not meant to make her more feminine, but rather to emphasize her masculinity. As she strode about with her spear, helmet, shield, and aegis, no one could guess that she had a softer, maternal side as well. It was not something she often showed—but it did occasionally emerge.

Hephaestus and Athena shared much in common. Both were interested in fine craftsmanship, he with his forge and hammer, she with weaving, carving, and sculpting. The two were often seen together, sharing information about some new skill or object. Alone among the gods, Athena's friendships with males was driven by compatibility, not physical attraction.

The gods, who often gossiped, said about Athena: "She thinks she is better than the rest of us"[1] because she rejected this type of attraction. On the other hand, the gods would reason: "She is Zeus' daughter. We know how he is."[2] They thought that since Zeus was often physically attracted to women, then Athena, being his daughter, must secretly desire to be with men on more than a friendly basis.

No one knows when it happened—maybe it was after hearing all the talk about Athena—but Hephaestus fell in love with her. Perhaps it was when he split open Zeus' head and Athena emerged, or perhaps it was because the two spent so much time together. When Athena

asked him to make new armor for her, it seemed to the lame god of the forge that this was his chance to be with her.

When Athena returned to his shop to get her armor, Hephaestus grabbed her. Athena resisted, intent on remaining pure of body. Because she fought back so fiercely, Hephaestus could not make love to her. Instead his semen spilled onto her leg. Grabbing a piece of wool, Athena wiped off her leg and tossed the wool out of the forge. It fell to the earth, where it impregnated Gaia (Mother Earth).

When the child was born, Athena took it and named it Erichthonius (ayr-ik-THOH-nee-us), which is a combination of the words for wool (*erion*) and earth (*chthon*). Perhaps Athena didn't want the other gods finding out that she was so attached to this child, because she placed the baby in a basket and gave it to the three daughters of Cecrops, king of Athens. Their names were Herse, Pandrosus, and Aglaurus.

Athena gave the girls strict instructions not to look inside the basket, but they could not control their curiosity. Herse and Aglaurus lifted the lid of the basket, intending to take just a swift peek inside. Who knows what they saw? Some say they saw a child that was half human and half serpent; others claim that a terrible serpent was wrapped around a human baby boy. The sight—whatever it was—drove both girls insane. They raced outside and threw themselves off the Acropolis, falling to their death below.

A crow, eager to tell Athena what happened, found her bringing back a huge rock to add to the Acropolis. When she heard the sad news, she dropped the rock, which became Mount Lycabettus. Then she turned the crow, which had been white, a color as black as night, and gave crows harsh voices because they were so fond of talking about misfortune.

Returning to the Acropolis, Athena took Erichthonius back. Some say that she tucked him inside her aegis, where he would be safe and warm. Under Athena's protection, the boy grew into manhood. Eventually he became the king of Athens, where he officially established the cult of Athena, instituted the Panathenaea, and led celebrations in her honor.

Athena and Bellerophon

It has already been demonstrated that Athena aided heroes. So it was with a man named Bellerophon (buh-LAYR-uh-fon).

Bellerophon was the son of King Glaucus of Corinth. (Some said that Poseidon, god of the sea, was his father.) Bellerophon wanted to control and ride the fabulous white winged horse Pegasus (PEH-guh-sus).

Pegasus had been born when Perseus cut off Medusa's head. From the blood of the Gorgon monster that seeped into the ground, Pegasus arose. Every male in Greece wanted to ride this fabulous creature, but no one could. Whenever a human approached Pegasus, he would snort and whinny, then fly away on his great wings. Nobody could get close to him.

Bellerophon went to the seer Polyidus (pah-lee-EYE-dus) and asked him how to conquer Pegasus. (A seer was someone who knew things no one else did.) Polyidus advised him to sleep in Athena's temple. As Bellerophon slept there, Athena came to him with a golden bridle.

"Asleep? Nay, wake. Here is what will charm the steed you covet,"[3] she said.

The next day, Bellerophon found Pegasus and approached him. The horse seemed about to fly away, but Bellerophon kept whispering in a soothing tone, and the horse stayed on

Athena aided Bellerophon in taming the mighty winged horse Pegasus by giving him a special bridle to use. Bellerophon's vanity got the better of him, and the remainder of his life was unhappy.

A Roman copy of an ancient Greek statue of Athena, whom
the Romans called Minerva. The statue features the aegis
bearing Medusa's head, and the spear and helmet that
symbolize her warrior nature.

the ground. Finally Bellerophon got close enough to slip the bridle over the horse's head.

Bellerophon had many adventures in which Pegasus played a vital part. One was killing the dreaded Chimaera, a monster who was part lion, part snake, and part goat.

Eventually Bellerophon forgot that the gods had aided him in his deeds, and that Athena had been the one who enabled him to tame Pegasus. He thought himself the equal of the gods because of his successes, and he decided to fly up to Mount Olympus to share their company.

Bellerophon slays the Chimaera.

This type of attitude angered the gods. As Bellerophon rose in the sky astride Pegasus, Zeus sent a gadfly to sting the horse. The horse bucked, throwing Bellerophon. He fell to earth and spent the rest of his days wandering aimlessly, because no one wanted to be friends with someone on whom the gods had turned their backs.

These are just a few of the many tales that feature Athena. A female who was not born from a woman's womb, more masculine than feminine, a warrior capable of exhibiting great tenderness, powerful yet surprisingly sensitive and compassionate, Athena was one of the most interesting and complex of all the Greek gods.

F.Y.I.

Minerva

Many of the Greek gods had counterparts in Roman mythology, and Athena was no different. The Roman goddess who was somewhat similar to Athena was Minerva.

Minerva was the goddess of handicrafts and wisdom. She also was a great protector of the arts. Among other things that she watched over were warriors, poetry, medicine, and commerce. She was also credited with the invention of music. One of her epithets was Minerva Medica, which signified that she was the goddess of medicine and doctors.

Her birth was very similar to that of Athena. According to the story, Jupiter (Zeus' Roman counterpart) had a tremendous headache. Vulcan (the Roman god of fire), like Hephaestus, was ordered to split open his skull to try to relieve the tremendous pain. When he did this, Minerva emerged from Jupiter's head, fully clothed in armor and holding a shield.

Another similarity to Athena is that, although Minerva was born wearing a warrior's armor, being warlike was only a small portion of her character. The warrior Minerva was only apparent in Rome. However, like Athena, worship of Minerva was widespread.

Thomas Bulfinch was a writer who popularized Greek and Roman mythology for nineteenth-century readers, just as Edith Hamilton did in the twentieth century. In his book *Bulfinch's Mythology*, he tells the story of Arachne and Minerva, which is exactly like the version with Athena.

Minerva

The main festival for Minerva, the Quinquatria, was held on March 19. According to Roman writer Ovid, the festival day was followed by four days of gladiator contests. A smaller version of the festival, held in June, was called the Minusculae Quinquatria. Along with Jupiter and Juno (who was similar to the Greek goddess Hera), Minerva was worshiped in a great temple in Rome.

CHAPTER NOTES

Chapter 1. Who Is Athena?
    1. Paul Hamlyn, *Greek Mythology* (London, England: Batchworth Press Limited, 1963), p. 31.
    2. Edith Hamilton, *Mythology* (New York: New American Library, 1989), p. 29.

Chapter 2. Origins of Athena
    1. Lee Hall, *Athena* (New York: Addison-Wesley Publishing Company, Inc. 1997), p. 21.
    2. Ibid.
    3. Ibid., p. 23.
    4. Ibid., p. 25.
    5. Jenny March, *Cassell's Dictionary of Classical Mythology* (New York: Sterling Publishing Co., 2001), p. 586.
    6. Hall, p. 43.
    7. Edith Hamilton, *Mythology* (New York: New American Library, 1989), p. 269.

Chapter 3. The Angry Athena
    1. Paul Hamlyn, *Greek Mythology* (London, England: Batchworth Press Limited, 1963), p. 32.

    2. Lee Hall, *Athena* (New York: Addison-Wesley Publishing Company, Inc. 1997), p. 57.
    3. Edith Hamilton, *Mythology* (New York: New American Library, 1989), p. 194.

Chapter 4. Athena and Heroes
    1. Lee Hall, *Athena* (New York: Addison-Wesley Publishing Company, Inc. 1997), p. 80.
    2. Edith Hamilton, *Mythology* (New York: New American Library, 1989), p. 145.
    3. Hall, p. 107.

Chapter 5. Other Tales of Athena
    1. Lee Hall, *Athena* (New York: Addison-Wesley Publishing Company, Inc. 1997), p. 78.
    2. Ibid.
    3. Edith Hamilton, *Mythology* (New York: New American Library, 1989), p. 135.

For Young Readers

Evslin, Bernard. *Heroes, Gods and Monsters of the Greek Myths*. New York: Dell Laurel-Leaf, 2005.

Ferguson, Diana. *Greek Myths & Legends*. New York: Sterling Publishers, 2000.

Hoena, B.A. *Athena*. Mankato, Minnesota: Capstone Press, 2003.

Osborne, Mary Pope. *The Land of the Dead*. New York: Hyperion Books for Children, 2002.

Spies, Karen Bornemann. *The Iliad and the Odyssey in Greek Mythology*. Berkeley Heights, New Jersey: Enslow Publishers, 2002.

Vinge, Joan D. *The Random House Book of Greek Myths*. New York: Random House, 1999.

Works Consulted

Cartledge, Paul. *The Greeks—Crucible of Civilization*. New York: TV Books, L.L.C., 2000.

Graves, Robert. *The Greek Myths*. London, England: Penguin Books, 1992.

Hall, Lee. *Athena*. New York: Addison-Wesley Publishing Company, Inc. 1997.

Hamilton, Edith. *The Greek Way*. New York: Franklin Watts, Inc., 1958.

———. *Mythology*. New York: New American Library, 1989.

Hamlyn, Paul. *Greek Mythology*. London, England: Batchworth Press Limited, 1963.

Johnston, Alan. *The Emergence of Greece*. New York: E.P. Dutton & Co., Inc., 1976.

Kravitz, David. *Who's Who In Greek and Roman Mythology*. New York: Clarkson N. Potter, Inc., 1975.

March, Jenny. *Cassell's Dictionary of Classical Mythology*. New York: Sterling Publishing Co., 2001.

Martin, Thomas R. *Ancient Greece—From Prehistoric to Hellenistic Times*. New Haven, Connecticut: Yale University Press, 1996.

Moncrieff, A.R. Hope. *A Treasury of Classical Mythology*. New York: Barnes & Noble Books, 1993.

On the Internet

Greek Mythology
http://www.mythweb.com/

The Immortals: Greek Mythology
http://messagenet.com/myths/chart.html

Encyclopedia Mythica: Greek mythology
http://www.pantheon.org/areas/mythology/europe/greek/

The Shrine of the Goddess Athena
http://www.goddess-athena.org

aegis (EE-jis)—The shield of Zeus and Athena, worn over the chest.

aristocrat (ah-RIS-tuh-krat)—A member of the class of people with rank and privilege.

bastion (BAS-chun)—A fortified place.

cult—a group of people bound together by their devotion to an idea.

decree (dee-KREE)—An order.

deity (DEE-uh-tee)—A god or goddess.

embroidery (em-BROY-deh-ree)—Designs sewn on cloth using needle and thread.

epithet (EH-pih-thet)—A descriptive nickname.

forge (FORJ)—The extremely hot furnace in which metal is heated before shaping.

hubris (HYOO-bris)—Excessive pride.

knead (NEED)—To work a substance into a uniform mixture by pressing, folding, and stretching.

loom—A device for weaving fabrics.

magistrate (MAA-jis-trayt)—A minor officer of the law.

nonconformist (non-kun-FOR-mist)—Someone who refuses to go along with established customs or thinking.

patriarchal (pay-tree-AR-kul)—Organized with fathers or other male figures as leaders.

prophecy (PRAH-fih-see)—A prediction.

tapestry (TAH-puh-stree)—A piece of fabric made of colored threads that have been woven to create a design.

valor (VAH-lur)—Courage and strength in the face of great danger.

whinny (WIH-nee)—The noise a horse makes.

ATHENA

INDEX